AND THE BONES STAY DRY

Michal Rubin

AND THE BONES STAY DRY

Michal Rubin

Copyright 2025 by Michal Rubin. All Rights Reserved.
Printed in the United States of America and published in Chapin, South Carolina. No parts of the book may be reproduced in any manner without written permission except in the case of brief quotations embodied in critical articles or reviews.

Library of Congress Number: 2025933835
ISBN: 978-1-942081-44-9

Cover by Molly Starin
Photography by Michal Rubin

Muddy Ford Press
1009 Muddy Ford Road
Chapin, SC 29036
MuddyFordPress.com

Contents

Part I

3	A child's night
4	Ben Gurion Boulevard
5	I see the seed-man's cart
6	1962
8	My father. On his death bed
10	My father's bones
12	I speak not your language she said to the boy
14	Useful

Part II

21	There Here
22	One flower emerges from the crack
23	Crumbled
28	Omar Abdalmajeed Asad of Jiljilya
32	Fifty minutes to sunset
33	Of bread and swastikas
35	The glass blower
37	You shall not destroy fruit trees by wielding an ax against them
39	Carolina Al-Tuwani
42	Statement on Water Distribution Policy in the West Bank, 2023
43	The Wall
44	In Gaza, 2014
45	Charlottesville
47	I am the field of their wars

49	Once there was a school in Jubbet ad-Dib
51	Non-Violent Communication in Four Steps: Instructions and Practice

Part III

59	Demolition— Hizma
60	Demolition— Beit Fajjar
61	Demolition—Al Fureidis
63	Demolition—Silwan
64	Demolition—Al 'Auja
65	Demolition— Deir 'Ammar
66	Demolition—Lifjim
68	Demolition —Duma

Part IV

73	I Would Like to Be God
74	Not now
75	Nice Words
78	Plum Red
79	Coffee with Allen Ginsberg
80	400 attackers, six arrested
81	God is tried in absentia
82	Meaningless
85	Exploits
86	Fourteen trees on Ben Gurion Boulevard or Interment
88	I Forget Time
89	I am told I must end a book of pain with love
90	Acknowledgements

*To all Israelis and Palestinians who have not given up on
the possibility of peace*

Preface

From the South Carolina patio I watch news from my other home, Israel, counting the dead after seventeen months of war. An ongoing trauma that engulfs homes, streets...land my feet knew so well, and the land of our neighbors, where my feet have not traveled.

The poems in this collection have been written throughout couple of years prior to the recent war, and are in no way an up-to-the-minute record of the events currently unfolding between Israel and Palestine. They are but my reflection and the expression of my own battle between my attachment to Israel, the home of my childhood, and my heartache over Israeli politics as it relates to the Palestinian people. I have long been torn between leaving Israel and loving it, while facing the truth and deceptions in the telling of its modern history. The poems weave a story of finding refuge and home of one peoples while losing refuge and homes for another peoples.

This morning, as I write this forward, the map of my wrestling is plastered on every news outlet, across social media, and on the faces of my friends and family. I recollect my childhood fears of my imagined atrocities of war as I sat in a bomb shelter, a twelve-year-old with my mother and our neighbors. Then later in the today, I face my very adult fears of antisemitism intermingled with my shame and pain of my country's behavior in Gaza and in the occupied Palestinian territories. The fears are no longer painted in muted, careful colors, but in garish bold cruelty. The visions of atrocities that were fears of a twelve-year-old, no longer are imagined fears but the reality of the savagery my people and our neighbors are drowning in. My poems are a telling of my small corner of the story of two peoples who have lost their way and continue to wander in the desert of the human shadows.

May we find a way to the humanity of each other.

Michal Rubin
February 2025

Foreword

It is very hard to live with silence. The real silence is death and this is terrible. To approach this silence, it is necessary to journey to the desert. You do not go to the desert to find identity, but to lose it, to lose your personality, to be anonymous. You make yourself void. You become silence. You become more silent than the silence around you. And then something extraordinary happens: you hear silence speak.

– Edmond Jabès, *The Book of Margins*

Faith, human decency, even despair—these are things that force us to enter a great silence and wait for it to speak. This impossibility is a living nerve in the poetry of Michal Rubin. As an Israeli Jew, she witnesses matter-of-factly to the reality of antisemitism. She has also, for many years, made the silence around the Palestinian occupation and oppression speak out. This is an untenable, truly an impossible, space to inhabit.

So it is that Michal Rubin's poems are poems of a most complex exile. As a human and as a writer, Rubin steps into and out of many forbidden territories. Her gift as a poet is to work creatively with the fact that she can no longer call any place or position "home." Rather, it is her grief, her outrage, her stubborn witness that furnish her with a home in language. Into that place of exile she welcomes us.

forbidden moment
fused with desert breeze

salted droplets we carried
home

*   or what was home*

This is not an easily classifiable book of poems. It could be called documentary poetry— certainly, I've never encountered a poem built around the four steps of nonviolent communication before, much less a poem embedded with links to newspaper articles. Attempting to quantify the loss of Palestinian villages, Rubin counts: "number of keys without doors: estimated 3,525." Recording incidents of antisemitism in the United States, she lists places and dates. Poetry, it seems is search and research, excavating the silences to make them heard. These poems also hold a poignant autobiographical element. Claiming the personal inheritance of her father's activism, Rubin insists that "orphaned ideas remain"—"they scrawl a homily/on justice and equality." Forging a way through these contested histories, the reader enters into a thorny haven, a site of stubborn attention and resistance:

in a world of remembrance

                              I fail to forget

the required forgotten

A proper condition of poetry, then, is generative heresy. Rubin simultaneously calls upon her own cultural and religious history while nurturing profound empathy for, and outrage on behalf, of a population most Israelis see as enemies. People who appear irretrievably divided may meet in the world that Rubin portrays. In pointed irony, the reader meets the Jewish refugees from the Shoah who refuse to accept a home from which Palestinians have been displaced. Later we meet a defiant Palestinian youth committing a vulgar act. This is humanity alive in conflict and contradiction. Justice may begin that simply—in acts of listening. To each protagonist, Rubin offers her keen attention: "you are telling your story."

I try to stitch words

so they become

an embroidery of unwanted

stories

At times, the poems lapse into a sense of futility, when it appears that "all is utterly meaningless." The poet indicts God. She feels that her stories are covered by gray dust. But then she resolutely walks back into the silence and makes it speak. She maps exile as a place where every story must be told, not just once but many times.

Before. I have written about this   before.

An empty lot that housed the school,

a house, a well, how many times?

One thousand four hundred eighty five applications

pleas for classrooms, bedrooms, toilets

Part of the heretical agency of poetry is its ability to enter into pain without resorting to the usual narrative solutions. Pain in these poems doesn't resolve, it insists. It insists on being heard, and it insists on listening to all that remains silent. A lesser thinker would find herself trapped here by politics and trauma. Yet, admitting that words "are steps on hot coals," Rubin says:

I rewrite I rewrite I rewrite I remember
         I revive the account of the crimes we commit.

Where do we find ourselves? Outside the bounds of easy answers, vulnerable to silence, fearful of permanent exile. Despite what seems like an insurmountable challenge, these gutsy poems use sorrow and anger to break down contested boundaries, thereby creating a space that includes all people.

So often our world bifurcates into apathy or extremism, yet these poems speak, unwavering and acute.

We must give our full energy to listening.

Elizabeth Robinson, author *Excursive and Thirst Surfeit*
July 2024

Part I

A child's night

A quilt.
I lie not alone.
The recording of Eichmann's trial a bedtime story.

I lie with my faded blanket hugging holocaust stories
in the company of testimonies. Pained voices.

Children brutalized, mothers watching,
one boiled potato to be shared, I lie with their hunger,

I lie with drawings of butterflies
"There are no butterflies, here, in the ghetto"
the poem reads —
I settle into a place where suffering is a virtue,

no longer alone, no longer cold,
wrapped in a quilt of holocaust.

A quilt.
Or a child's night.
Or I lie not alone.

Ben Gurion Boulevard

My feet hugged and pulled away from the concrete
sidewalk tiles pretending to be cool, walking barefoot
to the beach, the same beach where I want my ashes
scattered. The blisters a cushion, an added bounce
to my steps. I loved them. The sidewalks. The grout joints,
dirty, making sure to skip over. The blisters. The pain.
Spartan perseverance. Walking on hot coals. Words
are steps on hot coals.

And I throw more words into the mix.

My concrete. My sidewalk. My smoldering path. I knew it
like I knew the bottom of my feet and the street corner
where the blisters would be unveiled. Like words, or some
truths I can't hide. Eruptions. No more cushions, now sharp
objects, litter strewn on the edge of a tile, the stink of smeared
dog feces, unpicked, like stinging words no one wants to hear,
strewn on the page, waiting to be stepped on. And I throw more
words into the mix.

Stepping on hot coals.

My street. Its gray hue a blend of cracks and holes,
misconceptions, or simply lies about its smoothness. Unlike
the glazed stories I read in third-grade-book printed on
sleek paper with a flower at the corner. Still on my
bookshelf sixty years later. Like the smell of the bus fumes
permeating my barefoot walk. Still resting
in the recesses of my memory.

Words are steps on hot coals.

I see the seed-man's cart

He parks his cart at the corner of Reines Street and Ben Gurion Boulevard, his unshaven face unchanged from the week before. You never asked for his name. All you know is that he comes from an Arab village and you wonder if his son will be here today to help weigh the 150gr of salted unhulled sunflower seeds and 50gr of salted roasted unhulled pumpkin seeds that are way harder to peel and spit the husks, definitely not with the same efficiency as the sunflower seeds.

There is an art to eating unhulled sunflower seeds. The speed and accuracy of biting, the coordination of the teeth and tongue to crack the shell, fish the seed, chew it, and spit the shell accurately into the bowl. The dissolving salt, later mixed with the sip of grapefruit juice is the taste of Friday afternoon, as city buses begin their rest, the fumes land on the sidewalk, there is an emptying of sounds only to allow the 4pm news from the neighbor's radio to colonize the entering Sabbath.

Not good news. Usually. You continue to spit the hulls of the seeds, sip the grapefruit juice straight from the large bottle, and tune in to the names of the dead from the last terror attack. The pile of spent hulls in the bowl is growing. You look at it with a level of pride, for a moment think of the sunflower-seed-vendor from the Arab village who is so mild mannered and gentle. The 5pm news from the neighbor's radio penetrates the sip of grapefruit juice.

1962

The black rimmed glasses
on my father's bald head

matched his sharp words,
printed on newspaper pages, spoken

over loudspeakers, etched in me,
too hard for a nine-year-old to grasp.

*There can be no democracy
with social inequality,*

he said, and I nodded
we must promise equal rights

to Arabs and Jews alike, he said,
sitting in a circle with friends,

education should be progressive and secular,
I remember his declaration

*god didn't create the world, the bible
was written by people,*

the scripture I carried as I sat
back in a circle

on a Wednesday

chairs occupied with people
numb or just listening,

a few words were uttered, disturbing
the awkward silence that filled the room.

I sat there
with my silence and theirs

waiting for something
that did not come —

when the teacher asked me
How is your father?

a year later,

I had to say *he is dead* and the space was filled
with silence

which I break today writing to his remains.

My father. On his death bed.

A room. A single bed.
White.
White walls, white sheets,
white skin, white oxygen tubes
Small. I am small.
I have blue shorts on.
It is still warm outside.
I stare. I am afraid to stare.

Boi
karov e'lai
Come
closer to me

I wish he said. A whisper.

I barely hear it.
Steps. small. I am a child.
Nine summers he taught me swimming.

Al tif'chadi
Ani be'seder
Don't be scared. I am ok.
Sit here a bit. We don't have
much time,

I wish he said. A whisper.

Nine summers aren't enough.
He tunes in to his dying.
I mumble a goodbye
ashamed I can't say more.
I am nine
he is fifty-four

Al telchi. Don't go.

                                                I want
                                                more
                                                time
                                                with
                                                you,

I pretend he said.

I sit in the silence I fill
with a wish for the story.
The real one.

                                    Nigmar lee ha'zman
                                      It ran out. My
                                           turn.
                                      The story is alive.
                                      Find it, sing it,
                                      bear it, write it,

I can hear him say.

My father's bones

You just left

and there was nothing

but absence

permeating the hollowness

like the spaces between the bones
where flesh used to live

ideas remain

they rattle

a futile drumming against
                      the living brutality of today

       in what was
holy
land

they rattle

and the dog
howling over the pile   debris
remnant of a demolition

they rattle

You left without explanation

a shallow intake of air

and then
there was   nothing

but absence

unattached to the flesh of your children
orphaned ideas remained

they scrawl a homily
on justice and equality

rattling
a futile drumming against the dry

strewn bones

over the debris of demolished homes

over the tents of the evicted

over the stumps of olive trees

and the bones stay dry

in the valley

in the land

that used to be

holy

I speak not your language she said to the boy

I, born from the womb of
my mother's remembrances
wrapped in the cocoon
of her story.

                        You, amongst the
                        trees, the earth
                        below littered with
                        unpicked olives
                        the story of Hagar and
                        Yishmael
                        is your womb.

My skin a scroll,
an epic of what was,
a tombstone
etched with numbers.

                        The remains of the
                        broken down
                        home in the arid field-
                        your diary
                        carved in the stone.

                        You laugh in
                        pleasure,
                        your small act of
                        defiance,
                        your urine, naturally
                        marks your
                        territory which I have
                        marred,

I feel its warmth running down
my sweaty shirt
my tongue tied in shame,

                                        you are telling your
                                        story

I speak not your language
and it's 2pm
the radio announcer
reads out names of
lost relatives,
maybe they have survived,

                                        yours, they live in a
                                        tent
                                        somewhere
                                        without radio
                                        announcements,
                                        you guard the stones
                                        that have survived.

Useful

It is my feet that are marked with the imprint of the land.
They carried me with an obedience of a uniformed body,
though I was not one to be modeled after
as a fine specimen of a soldier.

But my feet were.

They took me to the places my reckless mind commanded,
bare or shoed. The feet obedient to my living in the love affair.
Land   feet   recklessness   obedience

truth.   I thought

of winter   my feet
squished onto
the soaked shoes
filled with first rain,

water

the cherished commodity
pooled
in the murky puddles
of uneven sidewalks

the galoshes stayed dry at home waiting for an opportunity
to be useful.

I mean,
a small new country needed us to be useful
always
and we were

usefully knowing names of trees and birds,

geographical details we collected
in Homeland classes,
skillful recitation of poetry in memorial ceremonies,

mostly
feeling at home

cozy with all that's familiar
and is just ours,

I thought

all that my feet introduced me to
as they carried me   through
remains of cultures,
where stones told stories

of two thousand years,
one thousand years,
five hundred years,
twenty-year-old stories.

The young and exotic stones
became homes
to new inhabitants,
there were no ghosts,

I thought.

My feet loved the sea, the one they wanted to drive us into
so we disappear,
the sharp edges of seashells   a reminder, but I laughed
and that was useful. To believe we will not disappear.

We are still sunning on the shores
of that sea, decades later,

laughter mired in the perpetual war—
but our presence

useful.

Part II

There	**Here**
The soccer ball rolled behind the pile awaiting the muffled footsteps chasing it grabbing its dusted skin left over from the rubble onto which it rolled.	The blanket is dragged on the concrete, underground it has a smell, she notices, learning to fall asleep with bombs in the background.

One flower emerges from the crack

                                    The dead lack such resilience

                    my grandparents

               my great grandparents

     my aunts

they were led outside of town

                their bodies fell

                        into the dug-out hole.

Crumbled
1948, Genya and Henryk—fractured testimony—

                promised   *an apartment,*
     they gave us
a key   *at Jaffa*   *near the harbor a house*
     we opened the gate   *couldn't*
believe our eyes...   *shock.*
The house   *beautiful*   *but*
    in the yard   *a round table* *set*   *dusty plates,*
    not for us   *...we were frightened.*
It hurt us,   *it reminded us*   *we had to*
leave   *everything*   *when the Germans arrived*
threw us into the ghetto.   *The same situation,*
        and it was not in us to stay...........
did not want to do the same thing that the Germans did.

my childhood storybook of imagined truth
     no longer in the museum
       yellowed in the naked sun
crumbled   gone to dust

no one
            dared
         to publicly speak
            of how Israel
       had expelled
                         Palestinians

1954
Israeli parliament
Constitution, Law and Justice   Committee
Chanan Rubin   member

Members   *wake up!*
my father's words
Hamatzav 'kmo she'neheva ein le'seto od

Unbearable   it is
     unacceptable   morally
the State of Israel,
    takes land away
        from those
who own the land.
Take it away,
profit from
    what's not
yours!

1960

No one

              dares

to publicly speak

        of how we

                had expelled
     Palestinians.

And Isaiah Spoke:

"For he [god] has said:
    small a thing   to be my servant
      restore   Jacob
Bring back   Israel

I will also make you light for the nations,
my salvation reach the earth"

You, Isaiah, promised

      make us the light for the nations.

You mock me with the
charm of your prophecy! as
the inconceivable clatter
of my people's swords cut
through olive groves
whose owners remain
behind the fences watching
our arms immersed in the
carnage of their land.

No one dared

                to publicly speak

                              Israel

did expel

                Palestinians.

I was so young.

2022

Israel's high court has ruled
    1,000 Palestinians can be evicted   land
repurposed
      military use,
                        single   biggest
expulsion

        Al Markaz village West Bank   the Najjar family
      they knew

              May 11

a neighbor called: *The bulldozer is coming*
                   the Israeli military had come
          knock down their house.

         The court   un-swayed

The Najjar's house   demolished,
the start   biggest mass expulsion
We had 30 minutes to get out what we could,   she said

     She looked over
pile of broken blocks   twisted metal her
family home

   It took no time and our house was gone.

According to the Geneva conventions it is
illegal
      to expropriate occupied land

             to forcibly transfer the local
     population.

The high court   green-lighted
    population transfer

Deportation of over 1,000 people set

                              a
            humanitarian
catastrophe

                   cementing military rule indefinitely.

I am

                   not young

                                      anymore

Omar Abdalmajeed As'ad of Jiljilya

Haaretz newspaper reports

3am
Omar Abdalmajeed As'ad is stopped by Israeli soldiers on his drive home, after spending time with friends.

the moon is smiling, oblivious to the rattled
heart thumping against the white shirt
buttoned tightly over a late-night dinner
of rice and maybe thick lamb stew

3:05am
The soldiers demand that As'ad step out of his vehicle. They argue with him for 15 minutes.

Hebrew and Arabic mingle in a snake-like dance
or a sword fight with only one sword
and one victor
always
the same one wins

3:20 am
The soldiers walk As'ad to an abandoned yard, where they handcuff him, lay him on the ground, gag him and blindfold him.

the rancid aroma of cumin and cinnamon, leftover
flavor of friends, permeates the thick
gag with a terrifying intimacy of living in a dream
of dying on the cold dusty ground

3:35am
Soldiers lead two more detainees to the yard. One of them notices As'ad is lying still on his stomach.

his full stomach is pressed against the small pebbles
as 78-year-old skin surrenders to the indentations
branding As'ad
declaring the kinship of man and land
as the almost full moon still is in oblivion

3:45am
Two more detainees are brought to the yard. No one is handcuffed apart from As'ad.

his hands bound to each other clutch fleetingly
moments stored in his wilting veins
toddlers joyfully
squealing   love making
lamb stew sweetness of pistachio-
filled baklawa

4:00am
The soldiers free one of As'ad's hands and leave the yard.

not bound together the hands no longer harbor
As'ad's stored moments
they "rest" upon the spillage of his life
leaving handprints
branding the earth
the kinship of land and man

4:09am
One of the detainees calls a doctor after noticing As'ad is unresponsive and his face has turned blue.

no flickering of the moonlight to mark
the moment As'ad's blindfolded eyes dimmed
the absence of air bluing
the wrinkled face

stillness

4:10am
A doctor arrives at the yard from a nearby clinic and tries to resuscitate As'ad.

the white shirt ripped   dusted
with the land no longer white
and new hands part the sea
of stillness in a futile effort
to infuse life into
this body   an empty vessel

zip tie on its wrist

4:20am
As'ad is brought to the clinic and medics continue to treat him.

neon flares no more moonlight
frenetic world life-sustaining measures violent
clanking desperation against As'ad's bare chest
desecrate the holy stillness
of dying at dawn

4:40am
The doctor pronounces As'ad's death

One commander will be
rebuked
two subordinate company and platoon commanders will be
dismissed

www.haaretz.com/israel-news/.premium-death-of-80-year-old-palestinian-was-moral-lapse-israeli-military-report-says-

As'ad is buried in his village Jiljilya

Fifty minutes to sunset

they appear down the hill onto his land.
Sticks   metal pipes   M16 no faces   eyes intent
piercing the air. He held onto his hoe   the sheep
scurry away   his feet planted,   an olive tree,   his land,
he is no sheep   someone's phone documents
the late afternoon in South Hebron hills   terror paints
the story   in colors
          red river generations-old
          sun-bleached grass   trampled
          a distant bleat

His arms broken.   His hands empty, the hoe, capsized
on the ground   blood on someone's face
the ambulance parks   land uneven   tires slashed
no help   iphones document dimming lights,
men writing another chapter   new era of pogroms
Hafez Hureini, 52,   from the village of Al-Tuwani,
in detention,   his attackers are free
      broken arms   resting on lap
      Hafez between guards judge   courtroom
      dimming hopes   orphaned sheep

972mag.com/settler-violence-hafez-hureini/
middleeastmonitor.com/-west-bank-
Israeli-settlers-form-militia-in-occupied-Palestine/
"organized terror" the minister calls it and remains
on the sidelines watching land games in an amphitheater

        sun-bleached grass hardened land
        bleats distant and fading

Of bread and swastikas

The fresh loaves of bread piled on store shelves I stood
inhaling the aroma irresistible   heat of the freshness
a blanket I carry home into the kitchen its familiar
possibilities of rituals   butter cold   the chunks melting
bread and butter become one   an afternoon   a child
in Tel Aviv

today my eyelashes fan the fog off the memory

    Alaska   *Graffiti swastika was found in a play area at*
                           a Middle School.

    Alabama   *Etz Chayim synagogue was vandalized with*
                           graffiti swastikas and the messages, Gas them
                         all" and "Jew rats".

I touch the street in my mind   my feet feel the sand on the
shore of the sea, moments from the house salty air coats
my hair, it bundles with stickiness of Tel Aviv's humidity.
I go into those years that space the city its streets fusing
into yesterdays   tasting the bread remembering
the dripping butter

today the rancid chatter drowns the salted butter

    Connecticut *Individual received a text message*
                           with a pornographic photo and a message:
                         "Kill Jew scum"

    Florida   *A Jewish woman was verbally harassed by a*
                         man who told her "Six million more should
                         have died", and "What are you, a
                         fucking filthy Jew."

I settle into the acceptance of today   my droopy belly
wrinkles on my hands floppy skin no longer elastic and
fresh   like days on the beach my body doused with cooking oil
browning in the heat of Tel Aviv   the magic of adolescent
mind dwelling in the rhythm of
an adolescent country

today the cobwebs are dusted off the myth

Georgia *Several middle school students wore swastikas on their sleeves and displayed Nazi salutes at school.*

Louisiana *Jewish middle school student was told she should go back to the ovens when she said she was cold.*

enveloped in a Jewish dream   a land   six million names
collected in books fill the atmosphere with their stories
I get used to the pain swaying between memory and fantasy
I visit their world   then wash it off believing it is
no more

today the buttered bread is lost

Texas *A man with a gun entered Congregation Beth Israel in Colleyville during services and took three congregants and a rabbi as hostages.*

Pennsylvania *A man entered Tree of Life Synagogue and yelled "All Jews must die" then opened fire upon the congregants and killed eleven congregants.*

I devour the buttered bread with someone's nightmare
barracks hunger city bus honks I taste the salted butter
savor the crust reach for the other slice push away
intrusions the bread and diesel fumes a fog
paints the illusion that it is no more

today the bread is just bread   that's all.

The glass blower

I watch his silhouette
against the furnace.
Tawfiq, he said his name,
from Hebron.
An art fair
seventy-two hundred miles
from the last checkpoint.
His accent carries the taste,
the nakedness
his last strip search.

He forms the vase,
turns the punty.
His defiance blown
into molten glass
in the fire.
Blue and green
of the Mediterranean
become a dwelling
to his history
a sphere around his blown words:

my daughter
in 22 years
has not seen the sea

the roadblocks
no permit
nothing changes

"blown" like the chanted words
of well-meaning protesters
carried by the winds
to the nowhere of the desert

You shall not destroy fruit trees by wielding an ax against them
Deuteronomy 20:19

She spans her arms across
sharp edges of hills
they are smeared with blood
her leaves sway sweeping off
remnants of war

her spine thick with years
twisted with her stories,
grooves, rivers
in the landscape of her body
her olives dropping, burying themselves
back into the dream of rooting

with thousand eyes
hidden in the silvery
green dress, she sees
the young ones ripped out
their roots dangling
her sap black tears

        for the   uprooted   broken
        burned down chemically poisoned

You shall not destroy fruit trees by
wielding an ax against them

f

ifty-five years
one million
maybe
nine hundred eighty-eight thousand
olive trees
gone

in mourning
she spans her arms across
sharp edges of hills

Carolina//Al-Tuwani

I
On Yom Kippur
we say
*For the sins we have committed against you by resorting to
violence*
*For the sins we have committed against you by greed and
oppressive interest*
*For the sins we have committed against you by plotting
against others*

II
Friday.
A pot filled with soil
from a Miracle-Gro plastic bag
holds the Creeping Jenny
which adorns it,
a dress with its matching scarf
trailing
green
leaf after green leaf
a Carolina patio
six thousand miles from Al-Tuwani
A day after Yom Kippur

the water hose bursting with
pressure
spraying its abundance
as each leaf bows
engorged
green
joining its sisters in a
parade of beauty
six thousand miles from Al-Tuwani
A day after Yom Kippur

III
Friday.
An email bridges six thousand miles
in one click, a news story—
a water transport to
South Hebron Hills-
Al Tuwani-
The village
awaits water
from a tank clouded by dust
The southwest wind
sees not
the absence of abundance

six thousand miles from Carolina
A day after Yom Kippur

The imprisoned water,
locked in the dull tank
adorned with green and black
banner
"Access to Water for All"
a vision
a plea
an impossible demand
in South Hebron Hills

Water is permitted on
Tuesday, Wednesday and Thursday

Today is Friday
A day after Yom Kippur

IV
I sink into the green of
the Carolina patio
hiding in the humidity
of shame
six thousand miles from Al-Tuwani
the Friday after Yom Kippur
For the sins we are committing against You
I mumble

Statement on Water Distribution Policy in the West Bank, 2023

In a whisper, the water spoke to the soldier,
a shy coolness, having lived in a pipe,
long time flowing. The soldier held the saw,
cutting teeth of the blade exposed in a smile,

a shy coolness, having lived in a pipe,
seeping from the jagged mouth of the pipe,
cutting teeth of the blade exposed in a smile,
water soaked into the land, bleeding,

seeping from the jagged mouth of the pipe
whispering, banished water tickles the cutter's shoes,
water soaked into the land, bleeding,
shoes tramp with disdain on the dark mud

whispering, banished water tickles the cutter's shoe,
a curse is muttered, the language of the water is muted,
shoes tramp with disdain on the dark mud.
Water's tongue blended with the earth where it is swallowed.

A curse is muttered, the language of the water is muted
with the flow. The soldier holding the saw,
water's tongue blended with the earth where it is swallowed,
in a dry whisper, the water spoke to the deaf soldier.

The Wall

        Adorned with barbs,
        a jeweled crown
        of separation

Red green black graffiti atop a field, rubber bullets, black
laying mingled Wednesday bullet next to Sunday bullet
cousins lay next to strangers history decorating arid soil

                she is cracked
                grooved
                pained

Yellow swaying dandelion   brushes against the gray

In Gaza, 2014

tomorrow's touch
through the settling dust

will remind you of
love

unhidden in the rubble
behind the corner

forbidden moment
fused with desert breeze

and grains of sand we carried
home

        or what was home

Charlottesville

an·ti-Sem·i·tism
/ˌan(t)ēˈsemәˌtizәm, anˌtīˈsemәˌtizәm/

Noun:
The act of inking yellow stars
and black numbers
on the horns of unborn Jew Babies

In a sentence:
Jews are a distortion of the human form

In a painting:
Long noses, hunched back, greedy eyes

In a song:
God cleanse America
the land that I love

In a drumbeat:
Right on hitler
Right on hitler
Right on right
on right on

Related words:
horns
leeches
roaches

On a map:
Americas *Asia* *Europe*
Middle East *Africa* *Oceania*

Morbidity: *Deadly*
Prognosis: *Immortal*

I am the field of their wars

sandal-wrapped feet
steps draw
the path
upon me
thus I am known

                          and taken
                          and fought over
                          grabbed in a fist
                          clutched by hand

they want me
I bear the weight
their yearning
I soak up their blood
and stay arid

                        I am the witness
                        the lover
                        the stolen
                        the given
                        the taken

                        the promised

                        the object
                        the prize
                        lost and
                        found

        sandal-wrapped
        feet draw
        upon me

         take me
         share me
         steal me
         dream of me
         leave me

I speak
with my breath
they don't hear

         I am the witness
         the prize
         the lover
         the stolen
         the given
         the taken

I am the mother of
Abel and Cain
Yishma–el and Yitzchak
the storyteller
of their lives
I am the field
of their wars

         I am the womb
         of their graves.

Once there was a school in Jubbet ab-Dib

***

On Thursday she watched from her shack
she smiled   some were late to class
holding the half eaten ka'ak Al-Quds still warm
she imagined za'atar on their lips

***

Five windows,
five doors,
five classrooms
a tree, flowers, painted on plastered school wall,
a playground,   simple,   a donation

***

On Thursday she watched from her shack
she smiled they look tired she thought
the soccer ball rolled slowly towards
someone's home   the sun beating the road
life in slow motion   summer's heat

***

the muezzin's call braided with bird cries
on Friday   the school yard is empty
dust   undisturbed by their feet
doors shut   quiet   she missed them

***

muezzin's call braided with bird cries
Could I write this again?
the school yard, the dust, the children
doors shut or just no doors?

***

It was said
the building's owner had refused to engage with Israeli authorities
over the status of the structure
before

***

Before. I have written about this   before.
An empty lot that housed the school,
a house, a well, how many times?
One thousand four hundred eighty-five applications
pleas for classrooms, bedrooms, toilets

***

the poem repeats itself

***

one thousand four hundred eighty-five applications
twenty-one approvals
when we arrived we didn't find the school
Mohammed Ibrahim said

a graded empty lot   clean
as if a virgin ground

***

Nonviolent Communication in Four Steps: Instructions and Practice per Model Thinkers

1. Observation: avoiding emotive evaluation; observation is focused on neutral statements.
>I do, observe:
>When I tried your shoes on,
>laced them with your words
>*god is king* and
>*a good Arab is a dead one*
>my feet spoke to the fire
>its silence
>ate the soles of my shoes

Example of observation: I see/ hear/ remember/ - description of what happened.

>I remember sinking into
>an inherited land, a taken land,
>someone's land,
>and you say
>*at war there is a duty*
>*to kill*
>and
>*I prefer them dead*
>
>I saw your eyes
>locked in a dance
>with the fire
>
>*an eye for an eye*
>you said
>
>There was more, I remember,
>I follow the instructions to observe:

> *may their village burn, terrorists*
> words chained my feet, held them
> locked to your shoes
>
> *not mine* I screamed
> *I am not you, let me out*

2. Feelings: identifying the emotional response triggered by the observation.
Example of feeling statement: I feel empowered/surprised/devastated

> I felt taken/pulled/devoured/sunk into
> the pool of crud
> crawled upon, ingested
> by godly acid

An observation:

> you mention god

Feelings:

> not god, what god, I feel not
> god
> I feel not
> non-violent
> I feel frantic/distraught/rabid/godless

Observation:

> I scratch frenetically,
> peel your words off my skin.
> You erase people without a stutter
> "I prefer them dead" you say.

       I glare at the 4-step instructions

3. Needs: identifying universal needs and values, met or unmet, that drive the feelings.
Example of needs: belonging/safety/growth

       I need air
       an escape from the prison
       of your shoes
       I need to not be you
       nor attach to the shame
       that belongs to you

4. Requests: Presenting a doable, concrete, specific way that needs can be more effectively met.

       All I want is to fight
       your trash in my garden
       to fight
       and forget the instructions
       I fight with my tears,
       or words,
       with the memories of the pleasure
       of a fight,
       I fight with my truth,
       not quiet, not nice,
       I fight with seventy years,
       with the aches of tired bones
       I fight...

I give up the instructions

I scratch frenetically,
peel your words off my skin
I rip letter by letter
pull and stretch the tail of the y
in 'eye for an eye'
it doesn't let go
the words,
they are splashed over my body
as my breasts and belly become
the map of your hate

Part III

Demolition— Hizma

she stood holding a pillow
clutching the tail of her
shirt

peering through
the toppled window frame
open

onto the gray concrete heap
the edge of the torn red curtain
unveils

echoes of bulldozers wrecking
her father's hunched body
held

by the groove of dismayed land
a son's hand
resting

on dusty hair yearning
to fix his father's
brokenness

at a distance a soldier's bored
stare thunders upon the arid
hills

she stood holding a pillow
clutching onto the engraved memory

Demolition— Beit Fajjar

a pillow   torn red curtain   concrete heap

bulldozers wrecking

grooved land

broken

father   toddler   dismayed

framed within the toppled window, the soldier, grays with the dust,

bored

with the echoes

bulldozers wrecking

torn red curtain

the hunched broken father

and the girl holding onto

a pillow

Demolition— Al Fureidis

Town of Kafr al-Dik   a pillow   torn red curtain

concrete heaps   bulldozers wrecking

    a soldier's bored stare dismays the pillowy hills

        village of al-Diyouk al-Tahta   town of Anata

bulldozers grooved land

broken

Al Fureidis   bulldozers wrecking

father torn   Hebron   broken

toddler   hunched   over   a gray pillow

torn red curtain

Village of Jalbun

    bulldozers wrecking

framed within the toppled window

        soldier, grays with the dust,
bored,

with the echoes
    bulldozers wrecking

Khirbet Humsu   dismayed   broken father

girl holding onto   East Jerusalem

torn red curtain

framed within the toppled window

                soldier, sunburned, grays with the dust,
bored

scans concrete heaps

and the girl holding onto

a pillow

bulldozers   concrete heaps   Masafer Yatta village

bored,   the soldier, red faced, grays with the dust forgets hunched broken father

       bulldozers   toddler clutching dusty hair

yearning   Khirbet al Fakheit concrete heaps

Al Jiftlik Ash Shuneh   concrete heaps

Ibziq   concrete heaps

she stood holding a pillow

clutching onto

engraved memory

the soldier, grays with the dust,

bored.

Demolition—Silwan

Truth comes in early morning
no bed to lie in

to be demolished
gray print, gray paper

bulldozer creeps into its ravaging self
a suitcase lost in the rubble

girl holding a pillow
what died is in a heap

the soldier cursed with
echoes   wrecking

no door to exit
in his shroud

standing   bored
in oblivion

no power to object
beneath   death creeps in

Demolition—Al 'Auja

Fifty-two weeks—-Number of demolished structures: 957;
number of girls who lost their homes: 235;

> Grooved arid soil lay
> beneath the rubble holding
> silent displaced screams

number of women who were displaced: 258;
number of boys who became homeless: 276;

> echoes of wrecking
> shroud a wilted soldier's soul
> boredom masks brokenness

number of men whose houses were bulldozed: 288;

> gray rubble gray dust
> gray hair gray tears gray sunray
> rest on torn red drape

number of affected people due to demolished structures: 28,474; number of red torn curtains: ~ 2,015

> I write my red screams
> over crumbled soul of boy-
> soldier lost and gray

number of clothes-filled bundles; ~ maybe 3,000; number of keys without doors: estimated 3,525

> I dream of him bent
> torn red curtain receives his
> awoken brokenness

Number of concrete heaps: 957

Demolition— Deir ʻAmmar

somewhere in South Hebron Hills there is a girl
holding a pillow

a pillow, torn red curtain, concrete heap   remnants
fifty-two weeks nine hundred fifty-seven concrete heaps
my rage dances within the walls of Carolina's comfort

a broken father fills his pockets with his shame
gray rubble gray dust gray sunrays color the forgotten
I write my red screams in the deafness of here

the bulldozer has no pockets and no shame   wrecking
in the gray dust a soldier is cursed   being there is etched
the radio mumbles lies and I wonder how could they

a toddler son hunched over torn gray curtain
three thousand keys scattered on concrete piles
without doors

        dinner hummus labneh Carolina kitchen
        shards of sentimental food penance to the distance

somewhere in South Hebron Hills there is a girl
holding a pillow

Demolition— Lifjim

In the world of remembrances I refuse to forget

                    a girl holding a pillow in the
dust of the hills

(zachór)

                Remember: a positive commandment,
                to be performed continually.

remember Abraham, Isaac and Jacob
                        a broken father
remember the exodus
                        concrete remnants of
                              homes

remember the covenant
                        torn gray curtain
remember blood libels
                        bulldozer tramples over
                              red screams
remember what they did

                            wilted soldier
                            bored

in a world of remembrance
                        I fail to forget
the required forgotten

Rewrite

I regret to inform you

                                    words
don't make up for heaps of concrete

                                    waving a red flag
unacceptable sin offering for a torn red curtain

                                    your poems, ah,
will not be heeded

                                    the heart ache you feel,
sacrifices nothing.

Demolition— Duma

I kneel down to pick up
one red anemone I thought was there
the image of red gets buried
in the downpour
of gray dust.

Nothing is left but
a rewrite of stories
concrete heaps adorned
with the shards of something red
dance of mourning, yesterday's gray dust.

The wind moans,
someone paints a yesterday,
a house, a smile, a red window
an awakened truth in the predawn hiding sun.

No one counts tears
yesterday's laughter has no echo
the sun heats the rubble like a dry fire
ravaging life.

Stories are covered by gray dust.
They dwell where the house was where
keys to the toppled doors are
swallowed.

I rewrite I rewrite I rewrite I remember
      I revive the account of the crimes we commit.

Part IV

I would like to be god

standing near the bulldozer's wheels. God as a traffic cop. In the sandy intersection, in a dancing move, raising my hand, stopping the rumble of the motor. In godly magic, it stops. Asking kindly for the driver to step down if he could or even if he couldn't, hand him my hand, if god has a hand, to step down from the height of his power-seat. Look him in the eye and notice his something. I check with myself, if god has a self, what is it that I see. I do see a story, I want to see a story, or maybe I make up his-story. A family in a dark room, where he is a boy, and is small. Above him, the table so tall, unbefitting his smallness. Beneath the table, his small feet dangling, moving, fidgeting. I see, because I am god, that his torn sandal is flapping beneath, his scratched knee from yesterday's fall is still glistening with the oozing life of a wound. The voices are loud, overbearing. His voice, unheard and small and fades under the booming of baritones, and it is as if he is not there, just not there. I look at today's eyes, big, loud baritone eyes and I ask, I am god so I can ask, what is it like to be tall and substantial, hulking and destructive, bigger and stronger and crueler than

Should I stop now? With the story. Should I tell you that I am not god. That I gave that job up. That I believe the position is not filled. The god position, I mean. Need I say that the hills are godless, and there is no one to dance at the intersection and stop, with godly magic, the churning of bulldozer's wheels? What a cliche it is to rhyme upon demolished towns, rhyme upon what is broken down.

Not now

We challenge you to write about our people who were unjust victims, he said. She knew her own dislike of the pleasure of holding onto victimhood and the image of her grandparents hurriedly dragging themselves into their grave outside of the shtetl moved from right to left to right. She was in the challenge and sank into the confusion of where she was going.

Put one word in front of the other to let them know she understands their suffering   past and present mingle   their suffering   not now and she lost her compassion as she entered the photograph of the demolished homes and the bulldozer they drove into the Masafer Yatta village like the horses galloping into the Ukrainian village of her people, their hoofs a bulldozer blade.

Back and forth she moves with garbled words as the stories of deaths run into each other but not now   not now *There is a time for everything, and a season for every activity under the heavens* she remembers the line and lives only in reckoning with her people's rupture of cruelty   her people.

She melds in their shadows as they chant *Death to the Arabs* and her words rain drops in death valley evaporate disappear the chanting continues the bulldozer blade dances wildly on walls of others.

Nice words

In my dream I caught my voice,
held it in my hands,
felt its smooth skin,
then opened my palms
let it go,
the voice reverberated
in the air
on my skin
on my body

awakened

I remember

there was a school there is no school,
there was a house there is no house,
there is a rubber bullet in a child's eye,
there was a well, there is a hole filled with concrete,
there were curtains on the window,
there is no window.
there is a man and his family doused by sewer water,
there was honor in the white shirt,
there is a drenched shirt with shit splashed over it,
there is life in the morning, and a funeral later that day.

In my dream I caught my voice
held it in my hand
used it as a pen
tried to write
nice smart important words
that imply
that hint
words that don't bleed

metaphors
of pain

metaphors
of injustice

I pointed a little finger towards the dark
in my dream
pointed a finger at an idea
a point of view
a concept
a hint to an assumption
and the real stains remained hidden
in my dream
the real pain got dreamily cleansed

awakened

I am washed with shame
I yell at my dream
its nice words
lies
and I write

I belong to the ones who maim
I belong to the ones who demolish
I belong to the ones that forget pain
forget pain forget pain of the other
I belong to the ones who say death to the Arabs
I belong to the ones who say *a good Arab is a dead one*
I belong to the ones who say *Muhammad is dead.*

No more writing nice words
in my dream
I thought of the next poem to write,
of becoming a camera
etching an image on a page,
accurate,
reliable,
true.

Plum-red

Murky puddles bedazzle my path
        I stumble onto the vending cart
splashing yesterday's rainwater

the market girl   now a woman
        immersed in unsung
hawkers' chants

war-tired people molest
        childhood memories,
tarnish the plums' red

I grab the plum, hungry
        for yesterdays,
fingering the firm and smooth skin

the tale of our innocence
        clasped in my hand
I bite into the tarnished plum

its juices trailing
        down my arm,
stickiness of childhood charm

Coffee with Allen Ginsberg

I write in your America. You
peer through the grave
nod   waiting   and you call out

blossoms are falling in the heat of the sun
libraries are filled with tears
there is going to be trouble

When you were seven
your momma took you to Communist meetings
everybody was angelic and sentimental

in Jerusalem
my father spoke of stolen land and unions
he was reading Marx

After your mother died you walked
reading the Kaddish aloud
the rhythm the rhythm   you wrote
yitbarach veyishtabach veyitpaar veyitromam veyitnase

for my father no kaddish was said
maybe that was perfectly right
like your mother my father
didn't pray

Wrestling, you and I, with our own Americas you said
there might be a rising   there's going to be trouble
you knew, and in my keening I say
"There is a dying"

400 attackers, six arrested, *Hawara, West Bank*

Jewish calendar date: 5th of Adar, (the month of the holiday of Purim), the year 5783; Sunday, 26 February 2023

In the dark the phone call lights the numbers
100 wounded 1 death
400 attackers
6 arrested
that's all
it's dark

I sway between lit numbers and dark letters
that appear on the page
the poems the words
I dream of writing
they are gone
it's dark

my people rampage untold history
burn paintings of the past
they are me no disowning
I dream of words
they are gone
it's dark

a burning fuse birth a "holy" ground - the land
the promised land devours its people
and across the Atlantic ocean
I put words in drawers
they disappear
it's dark

god is tried in absentia

31 degrees north 35 degrees east/ the village of Ein Samia/ 178 people 78 children/ 40 years of harassment/ unbearable/ in the name of god's promise/ what god would allow this?/ /

birds tweet on my porch/ I think of the kippah my grandfather wore to honor the same god/ he still had it on falling into the mass grave/ god was not there to see/ what kind of god would miss this?//

the kippahs are knitted, I think/ held by a hair pin/ lest they slip off when the men beat up the shepherd/ the sheep bleat as they scamper away/ the shepherd is chased off his land/ god is nowhere to be seen//

there was no time to pack a bag/ my grandparents just stepped out and closed the door behind them/ not refugees/ later just corpses/ five years ago I said the first kaddish for them/ just words/ no god//

I want to say kaddish for the dead/ Ahmad Jamal Assaf, 19/ Warani Walid Qatanat, 24/ shot by Israeli soldiers/ Qabatiya town, south of Jenin/ I don't want to wear a kippah/ I refuse to show respect//

31 degrees north 35 degrees east/ the village of Ein Samia/ 178 people 78 children tear down their tin houses/ after 40 unbearable years/ beaten in the name of god's promise/ they leave/ no doors to close/
I do not wear a kippah//

Meaningless

Hevel havalim, hakol havel—Ecclesiastes 1:2
Perfectly meaningless, everything is meaningless

I

In Rabin's pocket they found a blood-stained
piece of paper with the lyrics
to the Song for Peace, *shir lashalom*
Not a piece of art
A forensic post-mortem detail
that will be sectioned and colorfully
highlighted in history books.

The last breath, so ordinary,
sing-along, popular in Israel,
death by guns, barely a news item,
shir lashalom, loved by everyone,
Rabin sang it with 100,000 people
then he was shot
then died,
   singing   dying   might be ordinary
as are hopeless hopes
prayers for the dead
and "Let the sunrise light up the morning"
hevel havalim, hakol havel
all is utterly meaningless

II

Was it a surprise for her that the thought
"All is utterly meaningless" slithered
upon her kissing tongue making a salival ruckus—
its dispiriting quiver she camouflages
by heavy panting

and so it goes for the long sweaty minutes
till cum comes
such a meaningful rescue from the delusion
of lovemaking

She knows that all is utterly meaningless
he thought it was love
she was making shopping lists
drifting in and out of the essay she was writing
about the meaning of sex in the times of Covid

in the postcoital conversation he spoke
of the utterly meaningless speech Trump made
in the morning

III

mumbled words information lecture on treating trauma
death in the backdrop
laughter inside
boredom with meaningless psychology
gratitude list is a tool she says from the podium
they targeted her   Shireen Abu Akleh   CNN said
a journalist
maybe   maybe not

I retreat into death
of hope for something

my mind wonders   what they did with her
vest that said
PRESS
or hat
or her underwear and bra
the mundane items of living

tomorrow it will be erased
moved to 4th page
covered by ads
and her articles will be archived
like blood stained
lyrics of song for peace
Yitgadal Veyitkadash
"magnified, sanctified" just ashen.
hevel havalim, hakol havel Ecclesiastes 1:2
all is utterly meaningless.

Exploits

I write with no address
or neighborhood
letters that belong to
the smoke of burnt homes
or piles of old shoes

I try to stitch words
so they become
an embroidery of unwanted
stories

we live them
the stories
we spit them as hulls
discarded shells of seeds
we feasted on

I, the betrayer of dogmas spread
stained uniforms on the page
I, the jailed soldier
braid sins into the chain of letters
words bathe in shame
each bullet finds a target
smoke of burnt homes fills the nostrils
I, the one who left,
weave what you call art
with the exploits
remnants of our crimes

Fourteen trees on Ben Gurion Boulevard or Interment

carry my ashes along the boulevard counting
the trees along the way as I did in the pre-ash
state
love me there at the shores of childhood
with the urn's contents eager to join the
sea
speckles on the surface of the water
disturbing the green and blue
calm
which coats what's beneath

the ripples sway the specks of me
a cradle hushing the surface
words
and I   slowly   speck after speck
sink down into where I was born
and was meant to
stay

engulfed by what I had
left

returning

to the salt-water

rinsing

the crystals off my folds
the speckles off the surface
of my life

rinsing
the reminders
of the distance
from the sea

I forget time

or the water beneath the waves
a lure into the depth of understanding
surprised as even water betrayed my trust

water beneath the waves
capable of hiding its intention
to exile me

take me away from the shore
to where I am a foreign body
unrecognized

it leaves me changed
sometimes shattered
exiled from my youth

and time appears to join the ruse
it flows without movement
it hides beneath my skin

it hides in the pieces of me
in the spillage of words
it hides

I collect my strayed shards
in the torn net of my hands
and time is watching

still hidden
it flows without movement
it appears to join the ruse

I am told I must end a book of pain with love

love in the gray fire

Love cuts through, love draws lines,
lines acidly etched,
etch the promised land,

land falls into itself.
Love gets buried,
gets buried beneath,

love in the gray fire

beneath concrete heaps,

heaps hold captives-
captive unspoken truths.

Truth upon which time folds,
folds into silence,
still,

love in the gray fire

Acknowledgements

I am grateful to all my teachers but primarily to my close mentors Toby Altman and Elizabeth Robinson. Their generosity, guidance, and non-wavering support has helped me find my voice and stay the course. I also have deep gratitude to all my friends, fellow poets, and especially my husband, David Reisman, who patiently and lovingly tuned in to hear my voice.

Thanks to the editors of the following journals for publishing previous versions of these poems:
Fall Lines – a literary convergence: "Meaningless"
Minyan Magazine: "Coffee with Allen Ginsberg"
Rise Up Review: "Carolina//Al-Tuwani"
South Carolina Bards Poetry Anthology, 2023: "Fourteen trees on Ben Gurion Boulevard or Interment"
The Last Stanza Poetry Journal: "The glass blower"
The Wrath-Bearing Tree: "I speak not your language, she said to the boy" and "Omar Abdalmajeed Asad of Jiljilya"
Topical Poetry: "Fifty minutes to sunset" and "Not now"
Waxing & Waning: A Literary Journal: "My father's bones" and "Plum Red"
Several of the poems also appeared in the chapbook *Home Visit* (Cathexis Northwest Press, 2023).

About the Author

Michal Rubin was born and raised in Israel and has been living in Columbia, SC for the past 33 years, working as a psychotherapist and a cantor. The impetus for her writing is the unending and progressively worsening Israeli-Palestinian conflict. Poetry is her path of wrestling with the intermingling of her attachment to Israel, her birthplace, and her pain and rage over the years of Israeli oppression of Palestinians, the occupation, and the war in Gaza. She lives with the complexity of having grandparents who were murdered in the Holocaust and being a member of a "tribe" who practices apartheid. Her poetry was published in *Wrath Bearing Tree journal, Rise Up Journal, Topical Poetry, Fall-Lines, The Last Stanza Poetry Journal, Waxing & Waning: A Literary Journal, Palestine-Israel Journal, The New Verse News, Writers Resist, Dissident Voice, Writers Launch, and Critical Muslims*. Her chapbook *Home Visit* was published by Cathexis Northwest Press in 2024.

www.ingramcontent.com/pod-product-compliance
Lightning Source LLC
Chambersburg PA
CBHW061802070526
44586CB00023B/2680